# A Little Faith

# A Little Faith

## poems by
## John Skoyles

Carnegie-Mellon University Press
Pittsburgh and London 1981

# Acknowledgments

Acknowledgement is made to the following magazines and
anthologies in which some of these poems first appeared:

The Agni Review, The American Poetry Review, The Ardis
Anthology of New American Poetry, The Ark River Review,
Chicago Review, The Georgia Review, The Iowa Review,
Ironwood, The Missouri Review, The North American Review,
The Ohio Review, Ploughshares, and Shankpainter.

In addition to those whose names appear on these pages, I'd
like to thank Michael Ryan and Michael Waters for their
friendship and advice.

I am grateful to the Fine Arts Work Center in Provincetown,
the National Endowment for the Arts, and the Corporation
of Yaddo for their support.

The publication of this book is supported by grants
from the National Endowment for the Arts in
Washington, D.C., a Federal agency, and from the
Pennsylvania Council on the Arts.

Library of Congress Catalog ard Number 80-70564
ISBN 0-915604-43-4
ISBN 0-915604-44-2 pbk.

# Contents

IV.

For my Mother & Father

Our ties to beings and things are so fragile
they often break without our noticing.

— Edmond Jabes

I

# This Business of Dying

I don't care at all who died today.
There's not a single reason
to list the deaths today.
Maybe my father opens the sports page,
or my mother a mystery novel
in New York this afternoon,
a place where on another day
I could follow death like a woman
into the subway, where death
is just a headline, where boys
light freezing derelicts on fire.

So let's forget who died today,
the families, their keepsakes,
the clumsy last breaths.
Because this afternoon I know
I've invested my heart in good places,
that if this woman drops off to sleep
right now I'll still be here exhaling,
feeling guilty but lucky,
like a man with no connections.

Because someone left for work today
loving his children, but cursing his life,
and some union men, on strike again,
lounged in a tavern,
lost count of their beers
as I've lost track of these hours,
this afternoon, the days I've run through,
and the woman who moved me
this far, so far from my death.

# In Memoriam

We stayed in a resort town that Easter
and walked the beach at low tide,
eyeing what was left behind.
I was with a woman
whose mother had just died.
She seemed less a daughter than a souvenir,
a keepsake bringing back
a familiar "Remember that?"

The motel recalled my room as a boy
where a dog slept beneath the bed.
Driftwood twisted on the walls;
we put out cigarettes
in an ashtray made of shell.

She kept thinking about the past
while I couldn't help
imagining her years later,
as you run into childhood friends,
and the rings of their parents
appear on their hands.

At night I read late,
listening to the waves outside.
The rising and falling was punctual,
obsessed, like the routine
of someone about to break down.
She slept a lot, said little,
and imitated, I thought,
some gestures of her mother.

I never felt like a man there,
and before turning out the light,
I left a glass of water
beside the bed,
as if it had been brought there
in the middle of the night.

# Evidence

I used to pray in furnished rooms,
rooms where only my conscience
waited up when I came in late,
but since I'm with this woman,
I hardly ever pray. I think of my childhood,
my parents back home, and maybe raising
a daughter like the woman beside me.
And I remember what it's like
to live alone, with nothing but fantasy,

and what living with a woman's like,
with its special loneliness,
and the two lives not that far apart,
like this world and the next.
Men and women with no place to go
make God less alone, and couples
walk the same streets as the homeless,
both having someone to point to
when asked what they did with their lives.

# If You Have An Enemy

If you have an enemy, picture him asleep.
Notice his shoes at the foot of the bed,

how helplessly they gape there.
Some mornings he needs three cups of coffee

to wake up for work;
and there are evenings when he drinks alone,

reading the paper down to the want-ads,
the arrival times of ships at the docks.

Think of him choosing a tie,
dialing wrong numbers,

finding holes in his socks. Chances are
his emptiness equals yours

when you thoughtlessly hurry a cashier
for change, or frown to yourself

in rush hour traffic,
and the drivers behind you

begin to remind you
the light has turned green.

# A Little Faith

Because your priests pray nightly, God,
they miss the hideous light in our eyes.
Because they hear you, they scorn the lovesick:
those with hearts to their ears like radios.

And the man who makes his daughter kneel
on beans, does he work for you?

I know that in some parish
a nun is flattened on a corner
by shadows swinging two-by-fours,
that sinners cut their teeth
on nightsticks and suck the tailpipe
of a hearse for lifetimes.

Even those near your kiss:
old men who hug each other casually in parks,
those at home leaving for a smoke
until their wives sleep:
when they look at the stars,
it's not you they're thinking of.

And although we thank you daily, God,
we suffer sex, and women bear our weight.
We lie down with each other
believing in you, who sold us
our ghosts for a little faith.

# Guilt

I know it's dark inside us.
I'm sure we all feel haunted
by an absence of light.
Don't think I'm a believer
in original sin, but that woman
putting her plants in the sun
imagines the deep carpets in hotel suites;
and the boy sorting dirty postcards
in the night is so close to his needs,
his body is an echo of the dark inside it.

I guess we all have a skeleton
in the closet, a secret
that drives us from the warmth of home.
Because under dim streetlights
the broken-hearted wander
from corner to corner,
and in theatres the abandoned
settle softly in the dark
like kittens at the bottom of a pool.

And although the priests are urging us
to confess everything we've done,
I think we're grateful
for what we don't know about each other:
the past that's with us like a grudge,
the guilt we're feeling and God knows why.

# Excuse for a Love Poem

It must have been the last drink
that made me feel like this.
A woman looking in a store window
stood the way you do;
a man drove a truck with a child
in his lap and somehow this touched me.

I saw everything with such affection,
it had to be that last drink
that made me think of love as a relief
instead of the relief of nothing to love,
and I flirted with a waitress to celebrate
but she never came back.

The women I thought about
always had someplace to go,
and guessing where you were today
only made me drunker:
the loveliness of being held,
the quiet in which you are reading.

# Funerals

From those I attended as a child
for relatives I hardly knew,

I became an expert
on altarboys who couldn't wait

to play ball, and vagrants
who wandered in to get warm.

Now they're the last occasions
I ever think about death.

Now if my mother tells a joke
her Uncle Louie used to say,

or I hear a laugh like his
in a stranger's throat,

it all comes back:
standing at burials,

well-dressed and shy,
stunned by the gathering

of wreaths and bouquets,
mounds of earth

the body had displaced,
and prayers about the paradise

of meeting God face to face.

# Dear John

It's wonderful to see you here again.
I heard you were half-dead from loving
someone back in Chicago,
but the part that's living seems twice as alive.
Yet you're a little pale
from standing in front of the mirror too long;
you have that sullen look
I've seen on men in love with the same woman.

Please remember that I've missed you.
You haven't been yourself lately,
you've forgotten who you are:
you're no star, but you're popular.
As a boy you always did what you were told
and all the teachers kissed you.

I was proud of you then,
for keeping those magazines in the cellar
and passing them around.
So when the nuns made you head
of the Boy Saviour Club,
all the kids said :
"Everyone thinks John's an angel."

And when you led the class in prayer,
keeping a straight face
even to your closest friend,
I loved you then,
and you're still the same today.
But it's funny seeing you here
in a room full of strangers,
and you'll be the last to leave
if I know you.

We've come so far to be near
each other today,
I'd like to say I love you,
but forgive me, I'm too shy,
and can only love you now
through someone else's eyes.

# The Sadness of Music

**1**

The sadness of love drives music
like a heart, small deaths surfacing
in songs we knew happy,
but later let us down.

It swarms the air, invisible,
and crowds dance to it,
not knowing the beat comes from their hearts,
though they break up awkwardly
when the music stops.

It's something to listen to while the police
seize drunkards, while sitting with women
who do nothing but agree.

**2**

My uncle knew the sadness of music,
how it kept time with his pulse.
One wedding, he danced himself a heart attack.
His last steps were gruesome;
my aunt let him slide to the floor.
The music hadn't even stopped
and she was a widow, not more than fifty
scrawny caresses left in her anyway.

3

And who wouldn't like to close his eyes?
No more debating between a good face
and nice body, drumming our fingers
out of boredom.

This is why rock'n'roll groups
drive their limousines off bridges.

This is why we're grateful
when desire takes our brains by storm,
after the anxiety of the dancefloor,
booze, and strange women.
Some of them are young,
their hearts dying
to give up their bodies.
Music wore the others down
to memories, like the records
they sweated over years ago,
in musty rooms where they give in
when the songs run out.

# Burlesque
### after Weldon Kees

The day the dancer in the loud red dress
tossed her hair and said "What else is there to do?"
I remembered what my father told me.
She looked into the mirror applying makeup
while the traffic lights went on and off outside.

What my father told me was this:
women look into mirrors looking for men;
blondes toss their hair indifferently all night
but finally settle down; changes of heart
flicker like the traffic lights.

We fall in and out of love in rooms
where women wearing makeup
reflect our fantasies and lust:
so we're to blame for whatever they become.
And looking back, how could we

have taken that dancer so seriously?
But the way to forget
how she stepped out of her dress
was something our fathers couldn't tell us.
The lights go on and go off.

# Past Tense

I put a spell on her
by holding back.
She wanted to leave
without me waking up,
and used her body
to lull us apart,
since kissing keeps
the eyelids shut.
She became another
thing I saved myself from;
and although I said the old things
over again, in bed alone
they made no sense.
So I watched the late show
where a spy gave up
the secret code too late,
and cracked;
and on the news
a car radio still played
long after the wreck,
long into the night
of a summer like this one,
when the bodies
don't get cold and blue,
but burn like the shore,
fanatically hot.

# Invective Against Blondes

The body, my darlings, yearns beyond kisses
and far beyond the distraction of a bed.

A white shower of wedding rice might end
the years of looking, the time you tried out

ballplayers, playwrights, the average guy:
men who slept better when you were gone,

and were not surprised to have heard you say
"While you were away I fell for Fred."

Be careful, already at their endless chores,
the wives of friends seem more or less alike.

And the body, my darlings, sleeps half its life
like a pet in an armchair, like an unhappy wife.

# Snowstorm in the Country

Things are bad: birds outside my window eat snow.
I'm surrounded by trees, and children in the orchard
bully each other by climbing high,
higher than the smaller boys
who pick at the rough bark and wander off. . .

And there's a girl in braids who needs a boost
to the lowest branch.
She stays below, covered with snow,
a cold and lovely figure in that world of boys:
their inspiration or their hatred of it, I don't know.

# Home

Each holiday the family gathered
Julia's migraine, Uncle Fred's
great thirst, threadbare nephews
with their bachelor looks,
and a grandmother in a corner
who cared less and less:
a straying ghost helped keep her
out of reach while the men discussed
their favorite brands of beer,
and her daughters knew the prices
on both sides of the street.

# The Passage

That passage I wanted to point out to you,
the one I thought would mean so much,
I read it over just now
and you're not in it anymore.
It belongs to me and what's missing between us,
a feeling I remember from other passages.
Where they came from I forget,
and who was involved then hardly matters,
because with them, as with us,
what we went through together
never led anywhere; you were right to leave.
We might have accused each other in words like this forever.

# Knockout

Sometimes two people together
cancel each other out,
and are left dizzy and alone,
as if hesitating outside an office door
where they might not be wanted.
Those seconds are so conspicuous,
slower than the whole long day,
just like that instant in a slow round
when a good left connects,
and the crowd so silent
before it sinks in
that even the aggressor takes a while
to follow it up. And who knows,
his opponent might want to be alone now,
now that the boredom of vertical life has tasted him,
pulling him down like a lover
the way God floored St. Teresa
so she woke up not recognizing anyone,
but content she went through
something glorious and came out even.

# No Thank You

Who'll be the lover of that woman on the bench?
If she wants to hurt someone, she can use me.

Did she mean it, or was she trying to be unforgettable?
If she wants to use someone, she can hurt me.

I'll use my manners to stay in one piece,
but I end up believing every excuse that I make.

I always sigh when I see a woman like this;
I don't know where it comes from and I don't know where it goes.

I thought I'd enjoy a beautiful day like today.
I took a walk in the park and then something like this happens.

# I Don't Want To Hear Anymore About Love

I'd rather watch the junkman
arrange his new piece of junk,
or remember the way I felt as a child
holding my mother's hand in traffic.
There's a certain trust in these things
that I like, a mindless greed,
an unanswered lust, the kind
everyone knows is dead,
but some poor soul keeps trying to revive.

So I don't want to hear anymore about love,
unless it's a particularly one-sided love,
possessive love, love immobilized
by need, love with no chance
of fulfillment, a love so helpless
and frail it can only be kissed
and put to bed,
a love that needs someone
to wake it.

III

# Nijinsky's Diary

### for Michael Burkard

The day I read Nijinsky's awful life,
I kept my mouth shut

when I might have offered advice.
Crowds bruised him like an idiot boy

whose mother said to play outside;
and he hung around the same bars so long

the joking with waitresses began to get serious.
When I spend time near a man like this,

I like to be quiet, nurse my drink,
and stay put, because he revenged

the world's desire for his body
by going mad; and I defend my silence

at his madness with more silence,
the kind Nijinsky loved

in the Count of Monte Cristo,
who made confinement in the dark

a routine nightshift,
a loneliness that perfects revenge.

# Mime

They said my grandmother
got wiser every year,
but I remember her
saying nothing, just shaking
her head. In those days
I imagined what she never said
as so painful and true
she had to keep it inside.
She lived by a window
I could feel from the street
where I joked with my friends,
but always more softly
in front of her house,
almost in mime,
to keep them from shouting,
and my moonstruck grandmother,
sorrowful and dumb, nodding
to her rosary for me, a good boy.

# A Mother's Love

I know that if I called today,
her iron would be wrapped
in its usual steam
while the soap opera
went on telling its old story
in black and white.
She'd put her plants in the sun;
dinner would be on time.

Whatever I'm doing:
last night's drinks
and jokes at my expense
souring the afternoon,
my newest plans
that let her down without thinking,
I'm sorry

as the only child
of a woman whose one hope
is constantly changing:
long distance, collect.
Her voice loving my voice even more
for some small agony I mention.

# Queens, New York

In the neighborhood where I was born,
my friends have stationed tiny saints
on the dashboards of their cars,
relics from classes at St. Joan of Arc's,
where nuns were married to a god
who seemed cruel, but possibly true,
like rumors about Sharon O'Rourke
who crossed her legs and blew smoke rings
toward the classroom ceiling after school.

We dreamt of becoming presidents
while our fathers fell asleep in chairs
after three beers, an eight hour day,
and nine innings of the Yankees on TV.
Each Saturday they'd visit barbershops,
trade tips on horses or the stock exchange,
and relive disasters like the crash of '29,
when bankrupt brokers jumped off roofs
and sank in the tar like dimes on a hot day.

Rush hour took everyone underground,
and on weekends we joined crowds
of families driving toward the shore,
sometimes stalled by limousines
surrounding a chapel that seemed out of place
for hosting a funeral on a sunny day.
The mourning relatives, dutiful and black,
darkened the sidewalk with lengths of shade,
as if the shadows of the dead were still alive,

like feelings we bury, but still kiss goodbye.

# Kilcullen & Murray's
### for Keith Althaus

I take the stool
between the fat lady
bellowing Sophie Tucker
and the Irishman's Al Jolson,
near the obliterating jazz
and the merciful bartender;
because with the clinics,
rest homes, and funeral parlors;
with the news,
and the news behind the news;
with these people who are disappointed
every New Year's Eve,
and who are always facing spring alone,
you get tired of being serious.

# The Lovers

Disguised as mothers or aunts, our lovers
sag where we leaned against them.
At times they feel forgotten,
stranded in a bartender's jokes,
victims of fresh rounds of laughter.
They shiver under sheets;
their eyes gleam at the ceiling like coins.

Bored with talk and sex,
our friends become fathers drinking.
The rooms we enter are old men's;
our bodies tick vaguely with desire.

When the lovers leave, they leave
their imprint in the bedding,
line our wives' wide stomachs like scars.

If we remember, it's in unfinished letters to sons.

# Sonny Liston

He saw it in his father's eyes;
he drank it from his mother,
and most of his life he tried
to keep it out of places
where other people noticed it.
If it showed on his face,
he smiled, and made a joke of it.

So what if everyone laughed
and went along with it,
because he found a sport
that almost taunted it,
but each night lying in the dark
he confessed he was afraid of it,
and the shadow boxing in the hall
boxed on, suspecting it.

# The Fo'c'sle

You don't remember the tavern
down the block from where you worked,
how we waited for you to pass
and swooned behind the window
like guppies in love.

We slammed our glasses down
for no reason but to point out
we were alone with the mahogany
that would cradle our foreheads
late into the night.

Because you made us weak
in the knees, the guys
who follow boxing put it this way:
hit the body and the head will fall.
You don't remember.

But we imagine we're getting to you
as to the superstar who ignores
a ruckus in the bleachers
but still takes it home with him,
beyond us, where we never see how.

# Man Working at O'Hare Airport

The way he bears the noise and cold
might be the result
of a home life like mine:
a trust that what we're doing
we are meant to do.

When I asked my father
why the sky is blue,
he said: it's an easy color on the eyes.
So I thought things are put here
to be easy on us,
like this mechanic on lunch hour

who closes his toolbox
and sits down in the wind,
saying grace to himself
the way he works all day,
among the emptiness of crowds,

silent when the world seems twice as loud.

# Doing Nothing in the Spring

I'm sorry it's spring;
we might have warmed each other all winter.
Now mothers take their aprons off,
drive their children to the shore,
and men of place leave for work
with a confidence that made my father
stand back and say:
There goes a man with a purpose.

That I have no purpose,
that my walk through the park
is pointless and I slouch,
these things seem more apparent in the spring.
Last winter I might have blamed the cold;
now there is nothing to blame.

I'm sorry it's spring because in winter
I would have told you everything,
and now I begin to lie
as we go for walks,
like one of those schoolboys
who loses his books,
afraid of the rate at which everything grows.

IV

# Longings

There are longings so shameful even puppies
put their ears back; that leave a widower
packing a carton of skirts, thinking:
I should have told her I loved her more.

And there are longings that make us
go out alone, for the anonymous
pleasure of a stranger's warmth,
envying the cats in heat who just shake

their tails under a parked car,
without memories of childhood, shame,
or the longing of the blood to beat
for a life beyond the heart's routine.

For a life beyond the heart's routine,
men and women live together, look out
at the rain, and call someone theirs,
but one dies first. The other lingers

like a child in an attic sorting snapshots
of the dead, as puzzled as those
pictured on the lawn that sunny afternoon,
a day kept dark and hidden in a tin.


2
These memories hurt, but we check
to see if they still bring pain,
like the widower inhaling timidly
after his first bad stroke,
coughing in rooms where he waltzed
with his wife each New Year's Eve,
surrounded by cookbooks, clocks,
and snapshots of a new Ford near the shore.
These trinkets recall small anniversaries,
carefully arranged, but coated with dust,
like crimson rouge on the cheeks of a corpse.

**3**

And there are memories so painful
we somehow neglect them,
like the echoes of our mothers
giving birth;
like dreams they can't remember
but still feel;
like their sons
who failed in school
and still smell vaguely
of erasers tugging at a sweaty page.

If we love someone more fragile
than ourselves, but hurt her
as the world hurts us;
if our lover on a corner
looking both ways into traffic
seems more cautious than before;
if we walk away
from an uncle's wake
feeling nothing
but desire for a distant cousin,

well, the heart
is capable of such betrayals,
the mind is gifted with forgetfulness:
a blank when something passionate
takes place, a ballroom
spinning in the brain
of a tipsy girl on prom night,
her corsage already pressed between pages,
alone with its fragrance
as bouquets sent to pay respects to the dead.

# Saturday Night & Sunday Morning
for Michael Sheridan

You've fallen asleep with a drink
in your hand, goodnight.
Dream about me, your other friends,
and remember we catch cold,
call someone ours, and look out
the window alone. Then wake your wife
when sunlight breaks, and chase
your daughters from the guest room door.
Let me sleep late.

Through the hangovers and growing pains,
I can't forget your youngest daughter,
upset at last night's late show
despite the thrill of the hour,
adult laughter, and a new face
telling jokes. She took the movie
so seriously, she said today on the phone
to her friend: there were funny parts,
but it was sad at the end.

# The Lilies

When the fog broke, I stood on the lawn
stupidly shaking the guts of a flashlight,
gathering worms that came up for air;
and then I remembered Kerry O'Brien,
who kissed Sister Grace under a statue of Christ.
On nights like this I overhear their lips,
the kiss that left them paler than the rest.
It was spring, when everything drips.
Even the lilies choking in chapels
were immaculate and wet,
serenaded each morning by the confessions
of schoolboys, and a priest
seething Latin under his breath.

# Father Colombo

As a boy I went to church each week,
and listed sins to my favorite priest,
a goodnatured guy breastfed in Brooklyn,

whose smile wasn't cynical or coy
like the grins of archbishops,
and when he talked to God

his lips were surprisingly passionate.
Later I heard he left the church,
became a widow's exotic pet,

and summered on islands
with cool millionaires;
and I hoped it wasn't true,

because when I pictured him kissing
the powerful and rich,
he began to disappear,

like God did
when I tried to imagine
he always was, and always will be here.

# A Brief History of the Moon

At one time men loved the moon.
Dripping sailors gathered on wet decks
to read her features
like a crystal ball.

Men driven mad
by her pale body
howled to possess her.
And when she answered,

her words were so pure
they made no sound,
yet everyone understood her denial.
Still, her body taunted,

revealing only parts at a time:
a curved breast
or clouded thigh
as she leaned against the sky,

a star half-buried in her hair.
Eventually men stopped staring.
They drank coffee and glanced
at their watches.

The moon floated
across the sky
like a lost balloon.
The seas grew unruly,

the women irregular.
She guessed she was getting old
and found it hard to look
at her reflection in the oceans.

Soon she gave herself over
to the desires of a few dull men.
It's all right, she thought,
that they didn't say they loved me.

She had been alone for so long.

# Once Or Twice

**1**

You never let me have you
more than once or twice.
I guess these things
don't mean that much to you,
and I don't want to say
they have to be meaningful
in some silly psychological sense;
but for me, at those times
watching your face,
for a moment each feature
took on a life of its own.
And I loved those little lives
in you, being someone
whose life is steady and controlled.
So it was a release for me
to see you lose yourself
passionately, once or twice.

**2**

Leaving your house one morning,
after a night with you,
I saw children dodging
each other's snowballs.
One said "Where did I get you?"
I mention this only because
I have nothing else to say to you,
and there's a chance this detail
might soften up your heart a little.

# Falling Asleep

I feel her waving from a speeding train,
and look over, suddenly alone
with the face of a clock,
the high beams of headlights
igniting the ceiling,
off-key drunkards swaying home.
She knows where she's going
and begins to breathe deeply.
I'm not going anywhere
and yet I feel missing.

# Hard Work

This morning I have awakened in New York
while the population of California still sleeps.
A woman I once knew very well
pulls the covers around her shoulders
in Los Angeles, while I buy the paper
and a coffee-to-go
in this city where we lived together.

This room was ours, we shared it,
and used to lie in bed and guess
who cried behind these plaster walls,
who stumbled on the stairs late at night.

This morning as I woke up in New York,
schoolboys at bus stops exchanged
the facts of life, and the headlines said
there's a plane crash in the south,
those passengers seated beside each other
gone to different cemeteries
without exchanging another word.

This room was ours, but I kept all of it,
daydream near the electric fan,
visit those tenants who kept us awake
and play cards with them,
sullen men with nothing on their minds
but the good luck that deals them
three of a kind, the bad luck
that makes them experts at bluffing.

# Close

There's someone between us: it's you
as a girl not used to being chased;
it's me thinking we're most alone
when we touch. And there's something
between us like light between worlds:
we can't see any better and the stars
make us forget we live in a country
where people speak to each other
mostly for profit. Whatever it is,
I can still see you through it,
like something sheer you once wore,
I can't tell if it's closer to you or to me.

# Thank You

Thank you for leaving me
talking to myself in your voice,
and thank you for everything I said
about your needing me.

And for my invention of so many pet names,
thank you. They could have been heard
only by someone in love, in bed.

And thank you for making me so aware
of the pain of something said,
and the pain of something not said.

And for stopping me from thinking
what might have been, thanks,
because when you think like that

you're already in the past tense
and someone's got to bring you out of it,
thank you.

## In The Depot

I thought I saw you in the depot
though you were living in another city.

I don't like to make mistakes like that,
and I didn't care for the panhandler

who mistook my confusion
for a bewildered out-of-towner's

and recited hard luck stories
for some change. Worse, he asked

about that look in my eye,
guessed something was wrong,

a beggar's ancient line,
but I was so stunned

by your sudden appearance
I forgot the brusque phrases

for keeping my distance
I'd practiced so carefully.

# Conviction

I feel most alone when someone
calls me by name. Even though
there are times I'm completely withdrawn:
when the woman beside me,
as she's speaking abstractly,
seems more alive than in bed;
and although her breathing reminds me
we'll be on our own sooner or later,
I feel most alone
when someone calls me by name.

When someone calls me by name
I want to turn myself in
for bearing my fingerprints
and a whole family's blood.
My hands twitch like the couple downstairs
swearing again they were better off alone.
And I remember hearing it sighed so often
"I love so-and-so dearly, but. . ."
I'm ashamed to be near you
while having mixed feelings.

When someone calls me by name I remember
the people who thought twice about me,
who repeat to themselves the names
they're attached to, from pleasure
or heartbreak. And I think of myself
only as proof of two people's love,
that took them beyond the reach
of their bodies and settled here somehow,
where I feel most alone
when someone calls me by name.

# CARNEGIE-MELLON POETRY

1975
*The Living and the Dead,* Ann Hayes
*In the Face of Descent,* T. Alan Broughton

1976
*The Week the Dirigible Came,* Jay Meek
*Full of Lust and Good Usage,* Stephen Dunn

1977
*How I Escaped from the Labyrinth and Other Poems,* Philip Dacey
*The Lady from the Dark Green Hills,* Jim Hall
*For Luck: Poems 1962-1977,* H. L. Van Brunt
*By the Wreckmaster's Cottage,* Paula Rankin

1978
*New & Selected Poems,* James Bertolino
*The Sun Fetcher,* Michael Dennis Browne
*A Circus of Needs,* Stephen Dunn
*The Crowd Inside,* Elizabeth Libbey

1979
*Paying Back the Sea,* Philip Dow
*Swimmer in the Rain,* Robert Wallace
*Far From Home,* T. Alan Broughton
*The Room Where Summer Ends,* Peter Cooley
*No Ordinary World,* Mekeel McBride

1980
*And the Man Who Was Traveling Never Got Home,* H. L. Van Brunt
*Drawing on the Walls,* Jay Meek
*The Yellow House on the Corner,* Rita Dove
*The 8-Step Grapevine,* Dara Wier
*The Mating Reflex,* Jim Hall

1981
*A Little Faith,* John Skoyles
*Augers,* Paula Rankin